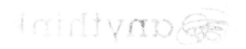

CRAZY CREEPY CRAWLERS

FLYING CREEPY CRAWLERS

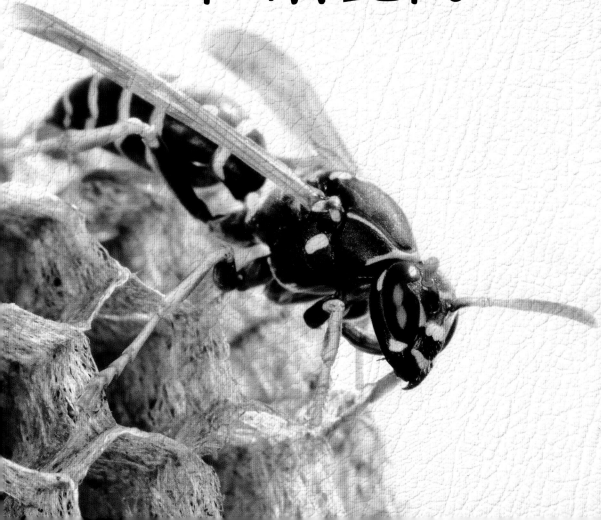

Thanks to the creative team:
Senior Editor: Alice Peebles
Fact checking: Kate Mitchell
Designer: www.collaborate.agency

Hungry Tomato™
A division of Lerner Publishing Group, Inc.
241 First Avenue North
Minneapolis, MN 55401 USA

For reading levels and more information, look up this title at
www.lernerbooks.com.

Main body text set in Calisto MT Regular 11.5/13.5.
Typeface provided by Monotype Typography.

Library of Congress Cataloging-in-Publication Data

Names: Turner, Matt, 1964– author. | Calle, Santiago, illustrator. |
Turner, Matt, 1964– Crazy creepy crawlers.
Title: Flying creepy crawlers / Matt Turner ; Santiago Calle, illustrator.
Description: Minneapolis : Hungry Tomato, [2017] | Series: Crazy
creepy crawlers | Includes index.
Identifiers: LCCN 2016022392 (print) | LCCN 2016024500 (ebook) |
ISBN 9781512415544 (lb : alk. paper) | ISBN 9781512430813 (pb : alk.
paper) | ISBN 9781512427141 (eb pdf)
Subjects: LCSH: Insects—Juvenile literature.
Classification: LCC QL467.2 T83 2017 (print) | LCC QL467.2 (ebook)
| DDC 595.7—dc23

LC record available at https://lccn.loc.gov/2016022392

Manufactured in the United States of America
1-39914-21384-7/29/2016

CRAZY CREEPY CRAWLERS

FLYING CREEPY CRAWLERS

Whoa!
Didn't see that
coming.

By Matt Turner

Illustrated by Santiago Calle

HUNGRY
TOMATO.

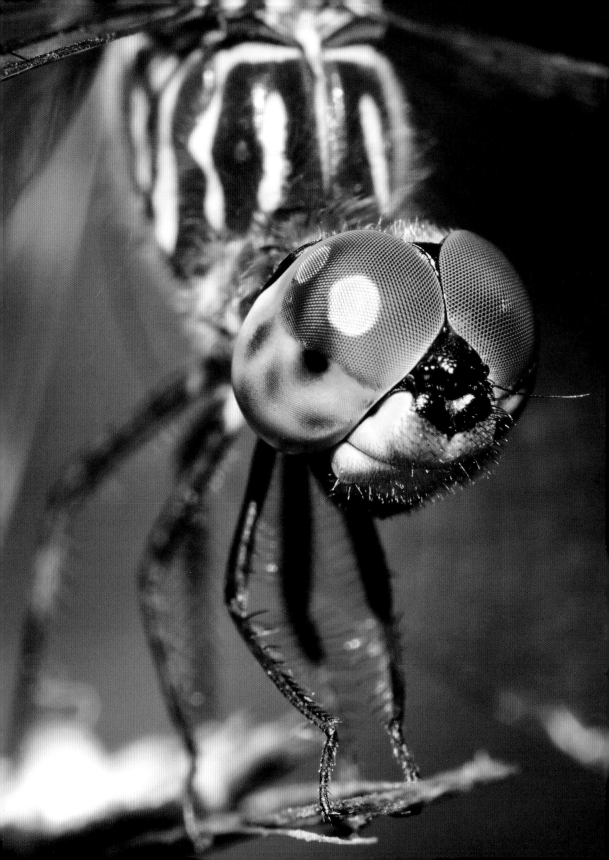

Contents

FLYING CREEPY CRAWLERS

Why did the first insects fly? You might as well ask why plants began producing flowers about 150 million years ago. The answer in both cases is "because it helped them survive." And in fact, plants produce their colorful, scented flowers to attract insects and other animals to pollinate them. The first winged insects appeared on Earth around 400 million years ago when plants began to grow taller and produce the first forests. So having wings enabled early insects to avoid predators and later to feed on pollen and nectar—just as modern bees, butterflies, and other insects do.

Wings are so important to insects that most of the major groups are named after them, using the Greek word *pteron* for "wing." For example, dragonflies and damselflies, which were among the first insects to fly, belong to the *Palaeoptera* ("old wings") group. These descriptive names can help us identify insects. Beetles (*Coleoptera*, or "hardened wings") keep their hind wings folded away under tough, protective forewings. Mayflies (*Ephemeroptera*, or "short-lived, winged") have a brief adult life, often lasting just a few hours.

Head   Antenna

Forewing

Thorax

Halteres

Abdomen

Leg

Winged insects can be amazingly big, beautiful, fast, or even dangerous—and they're incredibly diverse. The best part is there are many, many flying creatures out there—even in your own neighborhood.

Mega Wings

When a male butterfly courts a female, he hovers over her and showers her with perfume-like scents, which are called pheromones. This chemical courtship encourages her to mate with him. The male also chases away rival butterflies—and even birds!

Birdwing caterpillars taste bad! This is because they feed on toxic vines, and the poisons gradually build up in their body tissues, surviving right through to adulthood. They also have an *osmeterium*—a "stink organ" behind the head that helps ward off intruders like this possum *(above)*.

A birdwing pupa, tied to a twig by a fine silken halter, looks just like a curled-up leaf. This brilliant disguise helps hide it from predators.

About the only predator that will tackle a birdwing is the *Nephila* orb weaver, a very large spider that doesn't mind the bad taste of the butterfly's toxins.

BIRDWING BUTTERFLIES
These beautiful butterflies belong to the swallowtail group. With their long wings and strong flight, they have been likened to birds—hence the name. They are also the biggest of all butterflies. Queen Alexandra's birdwing, found in Papua New Guinea, has the largest wingspan: nearly 10 inches (254 millimeters). Thanks to the toxins in their diet, birdwings are rarely troubled by predators.

CAIRNS BIRDWING
ORNITHOPTERA EUPHORION
Lifespan: up to 3 months
Size: body length 2.8 inches (70 mm)
wingspan 5–6 inches
(127–152 mm)

VIVID MALES
Rajah Brooke's birdwing is the national butterfly of Malaysia. Like other birdwings, the green-and-black male is more vividly marked than the female.

COLLECTION
There are strict laws about collecting birdwings, which are rare in the wild. Most species can be raised in captivity though.

HUMMING AND HOVERING

The hummingbird beats its wings up to 70–80 times a second while hovering to feed from flowers and gave its name to the hummingbird hawk moth.

Sphingids are big moths that are strong fliers. One sphingid is the white-lined sphinx of North America (*right*), which also hovers like a hummingbird.

In 1862, Charles Darwin studied a huge orchid from Madagascar and wondered what insect pollinated it. The moth (with a mega proboscis) was found in 1903.

The hummingbird hawk moth is an impressive flier, able to "side-slip" while hovering, in order to dodge predators such as this praying mantis.

Some flies have an extra-long proboscis too. When similar features appear separately in unrelated animal groups, it's called *convergent evolution*.

HUMMINGBIRD HAWK MOTHS

If you spot a bulky moth hovering in midair next to flowers, collecting nectar with its very long, thread-like proboscis, it's probably one of several moths in the *Sphingidae* family that have evolved superb flight skills. They include the snowberry clearwing or "flying lobster" of North America and the hummingbird hawk moth of Europe and Asia. Listen closely, and you may hear the wings gently hum.

HUMMINGBIRD HAWK MOTH
MACROGLOSSUM STELLATARUM
Lifespan: 7 months
(including hibernation)
Size: wingspan 1.6–1.8 inches
(41–46 mm)

HIBERNATION
In parts of its range, the hummingbird hawk moth hibernates in a cosy nook in a tree or rock from October until April.

REPRODUCTION
The female hummingbird hawk moth produces up to four batches of eggs in a year, laying them on bedstraw, the caterpillars' food plant.

LIFE IS SWEET

The queen honeybee *(center)* founds a hive and lays up to 1,500 eggs a day. Fertile eggs hatch into workers *(right)* that forage for food, clean the hive, and nurse the young *(far right)*. They also sting! Unfertilized eggs hatch into drones *(left)*, males that fertilize the young queens that will found new colonies.

Domesticated honeybees live in artificial hives, but their wild ancestors would have nested in tree holes and similar spaces.

In doing the figure-eight "waggle dance" for others in the hive, a bee shows the direction from the sun to find sources of nectar, pollen, or water.

Giant Asian cousins of the honeybee have a painful sting, but farmers welcome them because they pollinate crops such as cotton, mango, coconut, coffee, and pepper.

Bees are important pollinators, but they are threatened by overuse of pesticides and by Varroa, a parasitic mite that has recently spread.

HONEYBEES

Along with making yummy honey, bees pollinate one-third of all the crops we grow. These highly social insects live in a hive containing fifty thousand or more workers and drones, ruled by a queen. Using wax squeezed from their body joints, they build combs made up of thousands of cells, where they store their collected pollen, honey, and other food and raise larvae.

WESTERN HONEYBEE
APIS MELLIFERA
Lifespan: workers 1–11 months,
queen 2–5 years
Size: 0.4–0.8 inches
(10–20 mm)

DANCERS
After returning from foraging, bees perform "waggle dances" and other moves that tell members of the hive where to find food-rich flowers.

THERMOSTATS
By vibrating their flight muscles, bees can control the temperature inside the hive, keeping it constant whatever the weather.

FUZZY AND BUZZY

The bumblebee is an important pollinator of early-flowering crops such as apples. It gathers pollen in fringed pollen baskets on its hind legs.

A single queen founds a new nest each spring. She builds the starter cells from wax squeezed from her abdominal joints.

Compared to the orderly structure of a honeybee comb, the bumblebee nest is an untidy clump of cells built in a tangle of foliage or a hollow. The cells serve as honeypots, pollen storage, and brood chambers for larvae. Workers keep the nest tidy and remove any dead bees.

In the fall, gynes (young queens) mate with drones (males). The drones later die, and the gynes feed heavily, fattening up for their winter sleep.

A cuckoo bumblebee is a female that invades a nest, gets rid of the queen *(above)*, then lays her own eggs and gets the workers there to care for them.

BUMBLEBEES

Fat and furry, the bumblebee is a welcome garden visitor because it pollinates wild plants as well as crops. Bumblebees are social, like honeybees, but form much smaller colonies, usually up to around 400 individuals. Unlike honeybees, bumblebees can fly in chilly weather, so they mostly live in cooler parts of the world. But this means their colonies usually die off in autumn, and young queens need to found new colonies in spring.

BUFF-TAILED BUMBLEBEE
BOMBUS TERRESTRIS
Lifespan: worker 4–7 weeks, queen 1 year
Size: worker 0.4–0.7 inches
(11–17 mm),
queen 0.8–0.9 inches
(20–22 mm)

WEIGHT
Aerodynamic experts once calculated that bumblebees were too heavy to fly! But they had forgotten that air behaves differently around small bees than it does around big airplanes.

DUMBLEDORE
One old name for the bumblebee is *dumbledore*. Harry Potter author J. K. Rowling used it for her Hogwarts headmaster, whom she imagined humming tunes to himself.

Expert Engineers

You can identify a paper wasp by its long hind legs, which trail during flight. By contrast, a common yellowjacket keeps its legs folded up neatly.

Paper wasps often collect timber from old fence rails. Listen carefully, and you'll hear a faint crunching as they bite it off.

Breeding males and females gather at a competition known as a lek, where males jostle for a high-up perch, or fight. Looks are important too: females with the greatest number of black facial markings and males with the neatest abdominal markings are considered the most desirable mates.

Paper wasps prey on lots of different insects. In summer you may see them take caterpillars as a source of protein for their own growing larvae.

The parasitic paper wasp *Polistes sulcifer* cannot build her own nest, so she takes over other nests and forces the workers to feed her larvae.

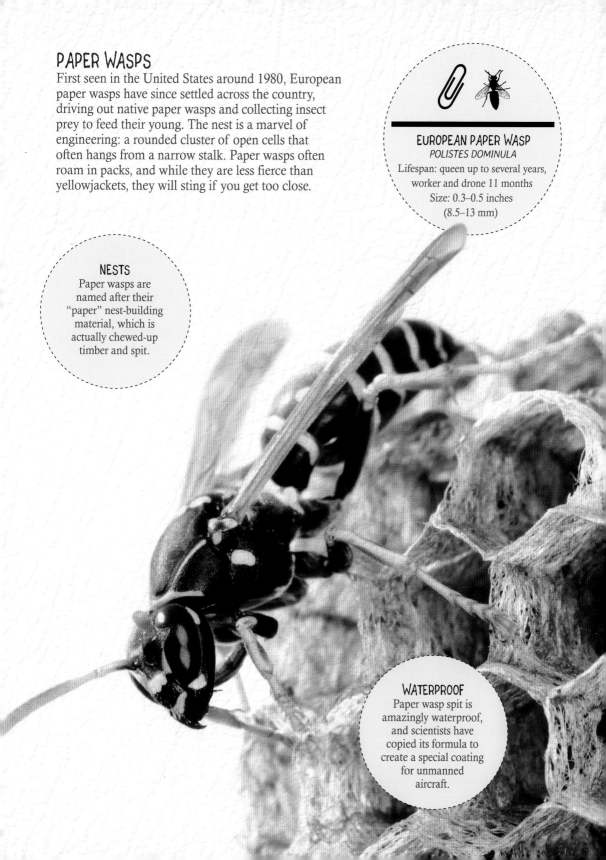

PAPER WASPS

First seen in the United States around 1980, European paper wasps have since settled across the country, driving out native paper wasps and collecting insect prey to feed their young. The nest is a marvel of engineering: a rounded cluster of open cells that often hangs from a narrow stalk. Paper wasps often roam in packs, and while they are less fierce than yellowjackets, they will sting if you get too close.

EUROPEAN PAPER WASP
POLISTES DOMINULA
Lifespan: queen up to several years,
worker and drone 11 months
Size: 0.3–0.5 inches
(8.5–13 mm)

NESTS
Paper wasps are named after their "paper" nest-building material, which is actually chewed-up timber and spit.

WATERPROOF
Paper wasp spit is amazingly waterproof, and scientists have copied its formula to create a special coating for unmanned aircraft.

BUILT FOR FLIGHT

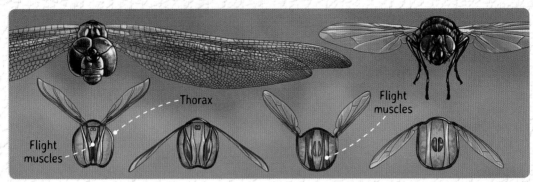

Thorax

Flight muscles

Flight muscles

The dragonfly's wing arrangement *(left)* is primitive but powerful. At its root end, each of the four wings is attached to a flight muscle for direct and independent control. A more modern insect, such as a housefly *(right)*, uses indirect flight: it deforms its thorax to flex the flight muscles.

I've got eyes in the back of my head!

A dragonfly's huge compound eyes usually meet at the top, for wraparound eyesight. Some dragonflies have wide-set eyes for better binocular vision.

He shoots . . . he scores!

Ouch

The predatory larva lives up to two years on a pond bed. It shoots out its mask (a hinged lower lip) in less than twenty-five milliseconds to snatch prey.

Where's he gone?

Male dragonflies are territorial, defending a patch of pond and chasing rivals away. The Australian emperor *Hemianax papuensis* uses motion camouflage, a special trick where he takes a flight path that makes him seem motionless to his rival, who can no longer pick him out from the background landscape.

DRAGONFLIES

Swooping and diving after their prey, dragonflies are excellent fliers, thanks in part to their all-around eyesight and also to the way their big flight muscles attach directly to the base of each wing. Europe's biggest dragonfly, the emperor, can hunt nonstop for hours over lakes and rivers, especially when there's plenty of sunshine to warm its muscles.

EMPEROR DRAGONFLY
ANAX IMPERATOR
Lifespan: adult usually 4 weeks, but up to 8.5 weeks
Size: body 2.6–3.3 inches (66–84 mm), wingspan average 4.2 inches (106 mm)

WINGSPAN
Damselflies and dragonflies form the order *Odonata*. The largest is the giant helicopter damselfly of Central America. Its wingspan is 7.5 inches (191 mm).

DIRECTIONS
A dragonfly can fly in any direction and even upside down when chasing prey or rivals. But due to the setup of its forelegs, it cannot walk.

Lightning Fast

A fly's halteres vibrate during flight and can detect any changes in the fly's pitch, roll, and yaw movements (up-and-down and side-to-side). The halteres send signals to the nerve tissues in the thorax so the flight muscles will constantly keep the fly steady. (If you want to see halteres, crane flies have a big pair.)

When you try to swat a fly, it calculates the angle of the approaching threat and within 0.01 seconds it has adjusted its legs to spring off in a safe direction.

Blowflies are often the first flies to lay eggs on a carcass because their maggots eat rotten meat. Police experts look for blowflies on a corpse to calculate when it died.

Because maggots only eat dead flesh and not healthy tissue, they have been used to clean up festering wounds—on soldiers in wartime, for example.

Scientists are researching natural chemicals in blowfly maggots. This may lead to new drugs to fight infections or even cancers.

BLOWFLIES

So how does a fly fly? In the true flies (order *Diptera*), the secret lies partly in the halteres. You can read opposite to learn how these clever gizmos work. Blowflies, meanwhile, are those metallic-looking pests that perch on fresh roadkill or on a juicy steak in the kitchen, laying their eggs and spreading disease. Their larvae—the classic horror movie maggots—have some uses in medicine that may surprise you.

BLUEBOTTLE
CALLIPHORA VOMITORIA
Lifespan: adult usually up to 1 month, but longer if it survives hibernation
Size: 0.4–0.6 inches (10–14 mm)

EVOLUTION
A fly flies only with its forewings. Long ago the hind wings evolved into halteres, a pair of knob-tipped stalks attached to the thorax.

REFLEXES
Why are flies so hard to swat? Partly because of their all-around vision and also because they think much more quickly than we move!

SWOOPING HUNTERS

Robber flies usually hunt on sunny days. They tend to wait on a plant, then zoom off and attack in flight, using their excellent vision and superb flying skills to zero in on the flight path of their prey. Spines on their strong legs help them grab the victim—and they always choose prey small enough to grab quite easily.

Many robber flies have evolved a warning coloring and appearance that helps them avoid predators. For example, this fly *(left)* looks just like a bee *(right)*.

The *mystax* is a moustache of bristles above the robber fly's mouthparts that protects its eyes from struggling prey.

A fly injects toxic saliva to paralyze its prey and soften its guts, which the fly then sucks up. The strong proboscis of a big robber fly can punch through a beetle's wingcases.

In one group of robber flies, the male has extraordinary hind-leg plumes, perhaps to impress a female during his courtship dance.

ROBBER FLIES

Not all flies feed on sugar, poop, and rotting meat. The *Asilidae* are a worldwide family of more than seven thousand species of robber fly: fast, powerful, day-flying predators equipped with stout legs that specialize in intercepting insect prey in flight and stabbing it with their needle-sharp proboscis. This injects saliva that paralyzes the victim and dissolves its guts. Not for nothing are they also called assassin flies.

ROBBER FLIES
FAMILY *ASILIDAE*
Lifespan: 1 year, maybe 2
Size: 0.1–3.1 inches (3–80 mm)

PEST CONTROL
Preying on ants, beetles, wasps, flies, grasshoppers, bugs—anything, in fact, that moves, robber flies are useful controllers of insect pests.

BIRD FOOD
Big robber flies like the bee panther *(Promachus rufipes)* or beelzebub bee-eater *(Mallophora leschenaulti)* have been known to attack hummingbirds.

FRAIL BUT DEADLY

A female mosquito can locate a host by sight but is also attracted by smells such as sweat and exhaled breath from as far as 164 feet (50 meters) away.

A feeding female injects saliva that keeps a host's blood from clotting and her proboscis from clogging. It's when the saliva is infected that she can spread disease.

A male's bushy antennae can hear the special whine of an unmated female's wingbeat. If they are compatible, the two mosquitoes will "harmonize," like two people who begin to hum the same tune, and then track each other down. It's a bit like having a built-in "find my mate" app!

Scientists took many years to realize mosquitoes spread disease. Medical pioneer Patrick Manson (1844–1922) tested malarial mosquitoes on his gardener, Hin Lo.

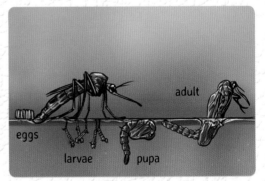

Most mosquito larvae develop in water, breathing at the surface and feeding on tiny particles. They also pupate and hatch at the surface, then fly off to find a mate.

MOSQUITOES

These flimsy little flies are parasites. The female sucks a host's blood to nourish the eggs in her abdomen. Some species also pass on diseases that kill at least two million people every year, making the mosquito the world's deadliest animal. And mosquitoes are terribly good at what they do: more sensitive to sound than any other insect, they create that awful whining noise just to find a mate.

MOSQUITO
FAMILY *CULICIDAE*
Lifespan: a few days to 1 month or more
Size: body 0.08–0.7 inches (2–19 mm),
average 0.1–0.2 inches
(3–6 mm)

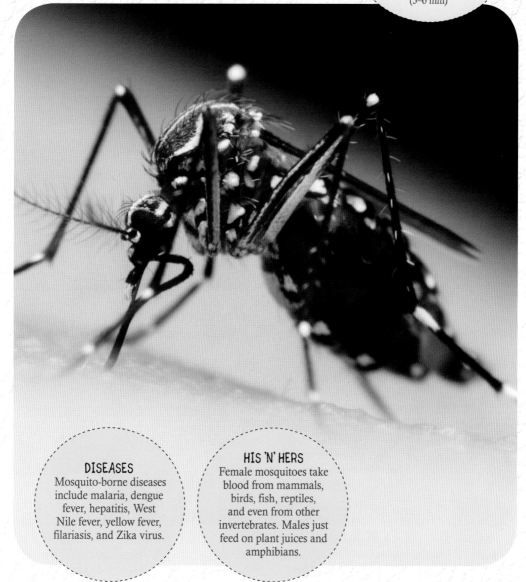

DISEASES
Mosquito-borne diseases include malaria, dengue fever, hepatitis, West Nile fever, yellow fever, filariasis, and Zika virus.

HIS 'N' HERS
Female mosquitoes take blood from mammals, birds, fish, reptiles, and even from other invertebrates. Males just feed on plant juices and amphibians.

INSECT ATHLETES

To jump, a grasshopper contracts two muscles in each hind-leg femur (the thick upper section) so that they pull against each other, storing lots of energy. Then, by suddenly relaxing one femur muscle, the energy is released and the tibia (thin lower section) can kick down to fling the insect skyward.

To attract a mate, a grasshopper makes a chirping sound, called stridulation, by moving its hind legs, rubbing them against notches on its wing veins.

Some grasshoppers are brightly colored to warn birds they are bad to eat. Others (above) will suddenly open patterned wings to surprise predators and buy time to escape.

Environmental changes can trigger grasshoppers to gather and migrate in huge swarms, devastating crops and even causing local famine.

Colorful grasshoppers are usually toxic, but the edible species are full of protein. Worldwide, around 1,400 insect species are included in the human diet.

SHORTHORN GRASSHOPPERS

Shorthorn grasshoppers don't really have horns—they have short antennae, unlike their cousins the katydids or bush crickets (with long antennae). The almost ten thousand species include locusts, which may form swarms many millions strong and strip a crop field bare in a few hours. While they can fly perfectly well, grasshoppers are far better known for their athletic leaping skills.

SHORTHORN GRASSHOPPER
SUBORDER *CAELIFERA*
Lifespan: adult 7–8 weeks
Size: body up to 6 inches (150 mm),
average 1.5–2 inches (38–50 mm)

GREEDY
It's estimated that, in a single day, a one-ton locust swarm can eat as much cereal as 2,500 people. In the Bible, a plague of locusts devoured Egypt's crops.

CATAPULTS
A grasshopper's hind legs are basically a pair of catapults, designed to produce leaping energy that is both rapid and powerful.

OTHER FLYING INSECTS

There are so many beautiful and fascinating insects in the world that one book isn't nearly enough to describe them—so here are just a few more.

Diving beetle: This big, powerful predator lives in freshwater, where it snatches other insects, small fish, and tadpoles in its sharp jaws. It breathes underwater by trapping a jacket of air beneath its wingcases before diving. At night, the beetle may spread its wings and fly from one waterway to another, using moonlight to guide its way.

Longhorn beetles: These beetles are named after their antennae, which in some species are even longer than the body—not that this prevents them from flying. One longhorn, the titan beetle, is one of the largest of all insects, at more than 6.5 inches (165 mm) long. Pictured here is the rare little rosalia longhorn of Europe.

Tolype moth: Moths are hairy, right? But have you ever seen one quite this hairy? You may see the gray caterpillars of the North American tolype moth infest fruit trees in spring. The superfurry adult then flies in search of a mate during summer and autumn.

Gotcha!

Cuckoo wasps:
There are some three thousand species of these beautiful wasps, which lead a solitary life, mainly in hot desert regions. Also known as jewel wasps, they get the name "cuckoo" from the female's trick of laying her eggs in the nests of another species. The larva, when it hatches, eats any other larvae in the nest and is then fed by the unlucky host adult.

FLYING INSECT RECORD-BREAKERS

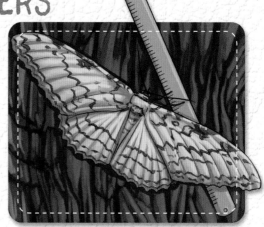

The largest swarm of desert locusts on record covered a 77-square-mile (200 square kilometer) area of Kenya, Africa, in 1954. It was estimated to contain 10 billion locusts.

What's the world's biggest moth?
That depends on what you're measuring. The Atlas moth (*Attacus atlas*) and hercules moth (*Coscinocera hercules*) have the greatest wing area but not the widest wingspan. That award probably goes to the white witch *(above)* (*Thysania agrippina*), an American species spanning up to 11.3 inches (289 mm).

The painted lady (*Vanessa cardui*) is not only one of the world's most widespread butterflies but its populations also make an epic migration each year. In spring as their southern habitat heats up, they head north as far as the Arctic. Then in fall as northern temperatures cool, they head south again, completing a round trip of up to 9,300 miles (15,000 km). But no butterfly ever makes the full trip. Instead, the migrant swarms go through several generations. In human terms, it would be like setting off for your annual vacation, dying on the way, and having your children's children's children finally arrive at the resort.

The world's toughest moth is possibly the Arctic woolly bear (*Gynaephora groenlandica*), which lives in the polar north. Its life cycle from egg to adult takes around seven years . . . partly because the shaggy caterpillar spends more than ten months of the year frozen, which leaves very little time for feeding! Uniquely among insects, the caterpillar can survive temperatures below –76° Fahrenheit (–60° Celsius), but to do so, it must pack its body with natural antifreeze chemicals before winter kicks in.

Glossary

abdomen — the hind part of an insect's three-part body

evolution — developmental change, from one generation to the next, in all plants and animals. The change is driven by environment. For example, if certain flower throats become longer, the insects that feed on those flowers are likely to evolve a longer proboscis.

invertebrate — an animal that has no backbone, such as an insect, spider, worm, or crustacean

larva — a juvenile that hatches from the egg and later transforms into a pupa or, more directly, into an adult. The plural of larva is *larvae*.

lek — a gathering where animals choose a mate, often by showing off their strength or size. It's common among some birds—but paper wasps do it, too.

parasite — a life form that spends all or part of its life cycle on or inside another life form, known as the host

pollinate — to carry pollen from one plant to another in order to produce new seeds

predator — an animal that kills and eats other animals. Roughly one-third of all insect species are predators.

proboscis — a tubular mouthpart in many insects such as flies and butterflies used for taking in food, often by sucking

pupa — a stage of development in which the insect larva rests inside a case and gradually transforms into an adult

social — forming a society in which individuals work together for the good of the group. Social insects include ants, termites, wasps, and bees.

thorax — the middle part of an insect's three-part body

toxic — containing poisonous substances

Buzzzzzzzzzzz

INDEX

The Author

British-born Matt Turner graduated from Loughborough College of Art in the 1980s. Since then he has worked as a photo researcher, editor, and writer. He has written books on diverse topics including natural history, earth sciences and railways, as well as hundreds of articles for encyclopedias and partworks, covering everything from elephants to abstract art. He and his family currently live in Auckland, Aotearoa/New Zealand, where he volunteers for the local coast guard unit and dabbles in painting.

The Artist

Born in Medellín, Colombia, Santiago Calle is an illustrator and animator trained at Edinburgh College of Art in the United Kingdom. He began his career as a teacher, which led him to deepen his studies in sequential art. Santiago, partnering with his brother Juan, founded his art studio, Liberum Donum, in Bogotá in 2006. Since then, they have dedicated themselves to producing concept art, illustration, comic strip art, and animation.

Picture Credits (abbreviations: t = top; b = bottom; c = centre; l = left; r = right)
© www.shutterstock.com:

1 bl, 2 cl, 4 c, 6 tr, 6 bl, 7 tr, 7 bc, 9 c, 11 c, 13 c, 15 c, 17 c, 19 c, 23 c, 25 c, 27 c, 28 tl, 28 bc, 29 tl, 29 br, 32 cr.

21 © Richard Bartz, Munich (Wiki Commons)